ESSENTIAL ELEMENTS

GUITAR ENSEMBLES

FIRST POPULAR SONGS

CONTENTS

Arrangements by Mark Phillips

ISBN 978-1-7051-7509-5

Visit Hal Leonard Online at
www.halleonard.com

World headquarters, contact:
Hal Leonard
7777 West Bluemound Road
Milwaukee, WI 53213
Email: info@halleonard.com

In Europe, contact:
Hal Leonard Europe Limited
1 Red Place
London, W1K 6PL
Email: info@halleonardeurope.com

In Australia, contact:
Hal Leonard Australia Pty. Ltd.
4 Lentara Court
Cheltenham, Victoria, 3192 Australia
Email: info@halleonard.com.au

CAN'T HELP FALLING IN LOVE

from the Paramount Picture BLUE HAWAII

Words and Music by George David Weiss, Hugo Peretti and Luigi Creatore

DON'T KNOW WHY

Words and Music by Jesse Harris

DON'T STOP BELIEVIN'

Words and Music by Steve Perry, Neal Schon and Jonathan Cain

FIELDS OF GOLD

Music and Lyrics by Sting

HALLELUJAH

Words and Music by Leonard Cohen

HEART AND SOUL

from the Paramount Short Subject A SONG IS BORN

Words by Frank Loesser
Music by Hoagy Carmichael

OVER THE RAINBOW

from THE WIZARD OF OZ

Music by Harold Arlen
Lyric by E.Y. "Yip" Harburg

SHAKE IT OFF

Words and Music by Taylor Swift, Max Martin and Shellback

THE SOUND OF SILENCE

Words and Music by Paul Simon

SWEET CAROLINE

Words and Music by Neil Diamond

WE ARE THE CHAMPIONS

Words and Music by Freddie Mercury

WHAT A WONDERFUL WORLD

Words and Music by George David Weiss and Bob Thiele

YOU ARE MY SUNSHINE

Words and Music by Jimmie Davis

YOU RAISE ME UP

Words and Music by Brendan Graham and Rolf Løvland

A SKY FULL OF STARS

Words and Music by Guy Berryman, Jon Buckland, Will Champion, Chris Martin and Tim Bergling